TRUST GOD'S PROCESS

From Caterpillar to Butterfly

Pastor Dr. Claudine Benjamin

Editor: Cleveland O. McLeish (Author C. Orville McLeish)

ISBN: 978-1-965635-96-4 (paperback)

Scripture quotations marked "KJV" are taken from the Holy Bible, King James Version (Public Domain).

About the Author

Pastor Claudine Benjamin is a passionate preacher, author, teacher, and prophetic voice committed to strengthening believers and equipping the church to walk in spiritual maturity and divine purpose.

With a ministry marked by depth, clarity, and spiritual discernment, Pastor Benjamin writes with conviction about transformation, endurance, discipleship, leadership development, and trusting God in every season of life. Her messages consistently emphasize biblical truth, character formation, perseverance through process, and complete surrender to God's will.

Through her growing body of published works, including books on spiritual resilience, divine timing, restoration, purpose, mental and spiritual health, revival, and the great commission, she challenges believers to move beyond surface-level faith and embrace the refining work of God.

Her writing carries a distinct prophetic urgency: to call the church back to patience in process, integrity in leadership, depth in discipleship, and unwavering trust in the sovereignty of God.

In *Trust God's Process: From Caterpillar to Butterfly*, Pastor Benjamin combines biblical wisdom with practical spiritual insight to remind readers that transformation is not accidental—it is intentional. Her heart is to see believers understand that hidden seasons are holy seasons and that crushing seasons often precede calling.

Pastor Claudine Benjamin believes that no season is wasted in the hands of God. Every trial, every delay, every silent moment is shaping something eternal.

Her mission is clear:

- To help believers trust God completely.
- To strengthen leaders with endurance and humility.
- To call the church back to character before charisma.
- To remind the broken that wings are forming.

She lives committed to prayer, discipleship, teaching, and writing messages that inspire faith, restore hope, and release courage.

Dedication

This book is lovingly dedicated:

- To every believer who has ever felt hidden.
- To the one who prayed in silence and wondered if heaven heard.
- To the one who obeyed God in obscurity while others were celebrated.
- To the one who endured crushing seasons and questioned whether the pain had purpose.
- To the one who felt dismantled, delayed, overlooked, or forgotten.

You were never buried. You were being built.

I dedicate this work to those in the cocoon season—the unseen season, the stretching season, and the breaking season. May you discover that what feels like confinement is actually construction. May you find the courage to remain when impatience whispers to run. May you trust that the silence is sacred and the struggle is strengthening your wings.

- To leaders who are developing in private
- To pastors who are serving faithfully without applause
- To intercessors who war in the unseen realm
- To parents shaping generations in quiet obedience

- To mentors raising spiritual sons and daughters through process…

…your hidden labor is not wasted. God sees you. Hebrews 6:10 reminds us: **"For God is not unrighteous to forget your work and labour of love."** He has not forgotten.

I also dedicate this book to the church. May we return to honoring process over performance. May we value character over charisma. May we cultivate maturity before promotion. May we learn to wait on God without fear. May we trust that divine timing produces lasting fruit.

And above all, this book is dedicated to the Lord Jesus Christ—the Author and Finisher of our faith (**see Hebrews 12:2**); the One who endured the cross before receiving the crown; the One who demonstrated that crushing precedes glory; the One who teaches us that resurrection follows surrender. To Him be all glory for every crawling season, every cocoon moment, every crushing experience, and every flight He has allowed.

To the reader: *Stay in the process. Wings are forming.*

Table of Contents

About the Author...iii

Dedication v

Introduction: You Are Not Stuck — You Are Becoming.............. 9

Part I

The Beginning of Becoming

Chapter 1: The Beauty of Becoming..................................... 17

Chapter 2: The Caterpillar Season — When You Only See the Ground.. 19

Chapter 3: Called to Crawl Before You Fly............................. 21

Chapter 4: The Appetite of the Caterpillar — What You Consume Matters.. 23

Part II

The Cocoon Season

Chapter 5: The Cocoon — Hidden but Not Forgotten................ 29

Chapter 6: When God Wraps You in Silence 33

Chapter 7: The Crushing, The Breaking, The Dissolving........... 37

Chapter 8: Trusting God When You Don't Recognize Yourself. 43

Chapter 9: The Danger of Leaving the Cocoon Too Soon........... 47

Part III

Strength During Process

Chapter 10: Emerging with New Wings 51

Chapter 11: You Cannot Go Back to the Leaf 55

Chapter 12: From Survival to Soaring 59

Chapter 13: The Butterfly Effect — Your Transformation Blesses Others 63

Chapter 14: Trust the Process — God Knows What He Is Doing 67

Part IV

Emergence and Elevation

Chapter 15: Having Patience During the Process 73

Chapter 16: How to Remain Strong While Hidden...................... 79

Chapter 17: Overcoming Discouragement During the Process ... 87

Part V

Commissioning and Impact

Chapter 18: Be Careful Who You Allow in Your Process Season 95

Chapter 19: When People Misunderstand Your Growth 103

Chapter 20: A Final Charge — Trust God Completely 111

Conclusion: The Process Was Worth It 115

Introduction

You Are Not Stuck – You Are Becoming

There are seasons in life when everything feels delayed. You pray, but nothing seems to move. You obey, but nothing seems to change. You wait, but nothing seems to open. You look around and see others soaring while you feel grounded. Others are advancing while you feel paused. Others celebrated while you feel unseen. In those moments, one dangerous thought begins to whisper: *Maybe I am stuck.*

But what if you are not stuck? What if you are in process?

THE MISUNDERSTOOD SEASON

The journey from caterpillar to butterfly is one of the most powerful demonstrations of transformation in creation. Yet if we only observed the caterpillar crawling on a leaf, we would never imagine the sky written into its design.

The caterpillar does not look like flight. It does not resemble beauty. It does not appear destined for altitude. And yet hidden within it is the blueprint of wings. So it is with you.

Jeremiah 1:5 declares: **"Before I formed thee in the belly I knew thee; and before thou camest forth out of the womb I sanctified thee."**

God's design for your life did not begin when you noticed it. It began before you understood it. The crawling stage is not a contradiction; it is a construction.

PROCESS IS NOT PUNISHMENT

One of the greatest misconceptions believers carry is that difficulty equals divine displeasure. When things slow down, we assume we have failed. When doors close, we assume we missed God. When silence stretches, we assume He is distant. But scripture tells another story.

James 1:2–4 says: **"Count it all joy when ye fall into divers temptations; knowing this, that the trying of your faith worketh patience. But let patience have her perfect work."**

Patience has work. Process has purpose. The cocoon is not evidence of rejection; it is evidence of refinement. The crushing is not abandonment; it is preparation. The silence is not neglect; it is incubation.

THE HIDDEN WORK OF GOD

Inside the cocoon, something extraordinary happens. The caterpillar dissolves. Its former structure breaks down completely. It does not gradually improve into a butterfly—it is entirely reconstructed from within.

This is what God does in hidden seasons. He reshapes:

- Your character
- Your motives
- Your desires
- Your thinking
- Your spiritual capacity

2 Corinthians 4:16 says: **"Though our outward man perish, yet the inward man is renewed day by day."**

While you feel dismantled externally, heaven is strengthening you internally. Transformation rarely feels comfortable, but it is always intentional.

THE TENSION OF BECOMING

Becoming is uncomfortable because it stretches identity. You begin to outgrow conversations. You outgrow environments. You outgrow habits. You even outgrow versions of yourself. And that can feel lonely.

Isaiah 43:19 declares: **"Behold, I will do a new thing; now it shall spring forth; shall ye not know it?"**

New things often feel unfamiliar, but unfamiliar does not mean wrong. It means growth.

YOU CANNOT SKIP STAGES

There is no shortcut from crawling to soaring. The caterpillar must eat. It must grow. It must attach. It must endure darkness. It must struggle to emerge. Every stage matters.

Ecclesiastes 3:1 reminds us: **"To every thing there is a season."**

If you rush a season, you weaken the structure of the next one. If someone cuts open the cocoon prematurely, the butterfly cannot fly. The struggle pushes necessary strength into the wings. Likewise, the difficulties you want removed are often the very things building capacity.

THIS BOOK IS AN INVITATION

This book is not simply about insects. It is about identity, surrender and trusting God when you do not understand Him. It is about believing that the delay is not denial, discovering that hidden seasons are holy seasons, understanding that your crushing is not your conclusion and emerging with humility and helping others through their process.

This book will walk you through:

- The crawling seasons of obscurity
- The appetite that determines growth
- The cocoon seasons of silence
- The crushing that produces oil
- The danger of premature emergence
- The responsibility of flight
- The call to strengthen others

It will challenge, confront and comfort you. But most of all, it will remind you that God knows exactly what He is doing.

A WORD TO THE ONE IN THE COCOON

If you feel hidden right now; If you feel forgotten, dismantled or delayed, know that you are not buried. You are becoming.

Philippians 1:6 assures us: **"He which hath begun a good work in you will perform it until the day of Jesus Christ."**

God does not abandon unfinished work, and you are His workmanship (**see Ephesians 2:10**). The cocoon may feel tight. The silence may feel long. The crushing may feel unfair. But wings are forming.

THE PROMISE OF FLIGHT

Isaiah 40:31 declares: **"But they that wait upon the Lord shall renew their strength; they shall mount up with wings as eagles."**

Waiting is not weakness. Waiting is strengthening. Waiting is stretching. Waiting is preparation for altitude. One day, you will look back at the season you thought would break you and realize it built you. One day, you will see that the very place you prayed to escape was the place that produced your wings. And when you soar, you will understand: *The process was necessary.*

BEFORE YOU TURN THE PAGE

As you begin this journey, I invite you to lay down impatience. Lay down comparison, fear and control. Trust does not require understanding. It requires surrender.

Proverbs 3:5 still stands: **"Trust in the Lord with all thine heart; and lean not unto thine own understanding."**

This book is an invitation to do exactly that. To trust the crawl. To trust the cocoon. To trust the crushing. To trust the emergence. To trust the wings. To trust God's process. Because you are not stuck, you are becoming.

Part I

The Beginning of Becoming

Chapter 1

The Beauty of Becoming

Becoming is rarely celebrated while it is happening. We celebrate arrival. We celebrate manifestation. We celebrate success. But heaven celebrates transformation.

The journey from caterpillar to butterfly is not instant; it is progressive. It is intentional. It is divinely ordered. Likewise, your spiritual growth is not accidental; it is orchestrated by God.

Philippians 1:6 declares: **"Being confident of this very thing, that He which hath begun a good work in you will perform it until the day of Jesus Christ."**

God is committed to finishing what He started in you. The caterpillar does not look like its future. It crawls low. It appears ordinary. It blends into its environment. Yet hidden within it is the DNA of flight. You may not look like your destiny right now. You may not resemble your calling. You may not appear powerful. But becoming is in progress.

Romans 12:2 says: **"Be not conformed to this world: but be ye transformed by the renewing of your mind."**

Transformation begins internally before it is revealed externally. The caterpillar must first grow before it wraps itself in a cocoon. Growth precedes glory.

Zechariah 4:10 reminds us: **"For who hath despised the day of small things?"**

Small beginnings are sacred spaces of preparation. Do not rush becoming. God is more concerned with who you are becoming than where you are going.

PRAYER

Father, teach me to embrace the process of becoming. When I feel unseen, remind me that You are forming me. When I feel unfinished, remind me that You are still working. Help me to trust that every delay, every pruning, every quiet season is shaping me for purpose. Develop my character before You elevate my calling. I surrender to Your transforming hand. In Jesus' name. Amen.

PROPHETIC DECLARATION

I declare that I am becoming everything God ordained me to be. I will not despise small beginnings. I will not rush divine development. God is completing what He started in me. My process is producing purpose.

Chapter 2

The Caterpillar Season – When You Only See the Ground

The caterpillar lives close to the ground. Its perspective is limited. It sees leaves and stems. It sees obstacles and barriers. It does not see the sky it was born to fly in. Many believers are in a caterpillar season. You are working. You are praying. You are serving. But you feel grounded. Ground seasons test humility.

Psalm 75:6-7 says: **"For promotion cometh neither from the east, nor from the west, nor from the south. But God is the judge: He putteth down one, and setteth up another."**

The caterpillar cannot promote itself into flight. It must grow into it. Your current season may feel restrictive, but it is developmental.

James 1:2-4 says: **"Count it all joy when ye fall into divers temptations; knowing this, that the trying of your faith worketh patience."**

Crawling builds patience. Crawling builds endurance. Crawling builds spiritual muscle. When Joseph was in the pit, he did not look like a prime minister. When David was in the field, he did not look like a king. When Jesus was in the wilderness, He did not look like a Savior about to change history. Ground seasons do not cancel destiny; they confirm preparation.

Micah 7:8 declares: **"Rejoice not against me, O mine enemy: when I fall, I shall arise."**

If you are low right now, do not confuse position with identity. You are not defined by your altitude. You are defined by God's assignment.

PRAYER

Lord, help me not to despise my ground season. Teach me to be faithful in obscurity. Remove comparison from my heart. Deliver me from frustration when others appear to be flying while I am still crawling. Build humility in me. Strengthen my endurance. I trust that this season is building me for greater heights. In Jesus' name. Amen.

PROPHETIC DECLARATION

I declare that my ground season is not my grave. It is my training ground. God is strengthening me in hidden places. My crawling season will produce my flying season. I will rise in due time.

Chapter 3

Called to Crawl Before You Fly

Every butterfly must crawl before it flies. There is no shortcut to wings. Likewise, there is no shortcut to spiritual maturity. We want elevation without preparation. We want influence without discipline. We want visibility without vulnerability. But God develops us in stages.

Luke 16:10 teaches: **"He that is faithful in that which is least is faithful also in much."**

Faithfulness in the crawling stage determines readiness for flight. Even Jesus submitted to the process. Before public ministry, He lived in obedience and obscurity.

Luke 2:52 says: **"And Jesus increased in wisdom and stature, and in favour with God and man."**

Increase happens progressively. The caterpillar does not sprout wings overnight. It eats, grows, sheds layers, and matures. Likewise, you must shed old mindsets.

Ephesians 4:22-23 instructs us: **"Put off concerning the former conversation the old man… and be renewed in the spirit of your mind."**

Before you soar spiritually, God removes what cannot fly with you. Some relationships cannot fly. Some habits cannot fly. Some fears cannot fly. If you skip crawling, you skip strengthening.

Isaiah 28:10 says: **"For precept must be upon precept… line upon line."**

Growth is layered. Trust the layering. Trust the shaping. Trust the refining.

PRAYER

Father, teach me to value process. Help me to remain faithful in small assignments. Deliver me from impatience. Strengthen me to walk before I run and crawl before I fly. Remove from me anything that cannot go into my next dimension. I trust Your timing over my urgency. In Jesus' name. Amen.

PROPHETIC DECLARATION

I declare that I will not skip stages. I will be faithful where I am planted. God is layering wisdom, strength, and discipline in me. My wings are forming. My elevation is coming.

Chapter 4

The Appetite of the Caterpillar – What You Consume Matters

Before the caterpillar ever enters a cocoon, it eats. And it eats constantly. Its growth depends on what it consumes. The transformation into a butterfly does not begin in the cocoon; it begins with appetite. Likewise, your spiritual transformation is directly connected to what you consume daily. What feeds you forms you. What you repeatedly digest shapes who you become.

SPIRITUAL DIET DETERMINES SPIRITUAL DEVELOPMENT

Matthew 4:4 declares: **"Man shall not live by bread alone, but by every word that proceedeth out of the mouth of God."**

If a caterpillar stops eating, it cannot grow. If a believer stops feeding on the Word, growth stagnates. Many believers desire transformation but neglect nourishment. You cannot feed on gossip, negativity, bitterness, social comparison, and carnal entertainment and expect spiritual wings.

Psalm 1:1–3 teaches that the blessed man delights in the law of the Lord and meditates on it day and night. That person becomes like a tree planted by rivers of water. Notice—meditation produces stability. The caterpillar does not randomly eat anything. It feeds on what is necessary for development. You must guard your spiritual intake.

Proverbs 4:23 says: **"Keep thy heart with all diligence; for out of it are the issues of life."**

If your heart is your spiritual core, then what enters it determines your future output.

YOU GROW TOWARD WHAT YOU FEED

Whatever you feed grows. Feed fear, anxiety increases. Feed offense, resentment multiplies. Feed faith, confidence rises.

Romans 10:17 says: **"So then faith cometh by hearing, and hearing by the word of God."**

Faith is fed. Doubt is fed. Discouragement is fed.

Ask yourself:

- What conversations am I consistently entertaining?
- What voices am I allowing to shape my mindset?
- What thoughts am I rehearsing?

Philippians 4:8 instructs us to think on things that are true, honest, just, pure, lovely, and of good report. Your transformation depends on your thought life.

The caterpillar grows quietly while consuming what sustains it. Your quiet growth is happening when you consistently consume the Word, worship, and prayer, even when no one sees.

STARVING THE FLESH, FEEDING THE SPIRIT

Galatians 5:16 says: **"Walk in the Spirit, and ye shall not fulfil the lust of the flesh."**

Transformation requires discipline. Sometimes God allows ground seasons to expose unhealthy appetites. Some people crave attention. Some crave validation. Some crave control.

Matthew 5:6 says: **"Blessed are they which do hunger and thirst after righteousness: for they shall be filled."**

What are you hungry for? Your hunger reveals your future. The caterpillar's appetite prepares it for metamorphosis. Your spiritual appetite prepares you for elevation.

PRAYER

Father, search my heart and purify my appetite. Remove every craving that does not align with Your will. Help me to hunger for righteousness more than recognition. Teach me to love Your Word more than worldly approval. Feed my spirit daily. Discipline my flesh. Let my intake reflect my destiny. In Jesus' name. Amen.

PROPHETIC DECLARATION

I declare that my appetite is shifting. I hunger for God more than applause. I crave righteousness more than recognition. What I consume will strengthen my calling. My spiritual diet is preparing me for divine flight.

Part II

The Cocoon Season

Chapter 5

The Cocoon – Hidden but Not Forgotten

There comes a moment when the caterpillar stops moving. It attaches itself. It becomes still. Then it forms a cocoon. From the outside, it looks inactive. But inside, it is undergoing one of the most radical transformations in nature. The caterpillar literally dissolves. Its old structure breaks down at the cellular level. It does not improve into a butterfly; it becomes entirely new.

GOD USES HIDDEN SEASONS FOR DEEP RECONSTRUCTION

John 12:24 says: **"Except a corn of wheat fall into the ground and die, it abideth alone: but if it die, it bringeth forth much fruit."**

Death precedes multiplication. The cocoon represents death to the old identity. Inside your cocoon season:

- Old ambitions die.
- Old insecurities dissolve.
- Old dependencies fade.

- Old fears are confronted.

But from that breaking comes rebuilding.

2 Corinthians 5:17 declares: **"If any man be in Christ, he is a new creature: old things are passed away; behold, all things are become new."**

Transformation requires surrender.

HIDDEN DOES NOT MEAN ABANDONED

One of the hardest parts of the cocoon season is invisibility. No applause. No visibility. No affirmation. David experienced a cocoon season while hiding in caves. Joseph experienced one in prison. Paul experienced one in Arabia.

Psalm 139:15–16 says: **"My substance was not hid from thee, when I was made in secret… Thine eyes did see my substance, yet being unperfect."**

God sees you in secret. Your hidden season is not punishment; it is preparation.

Isaiah 49:2 says: **"In the shadow of His hand hath He hid me."**

Being hidden in God's hand is protection.

THE BREAKING BEFORE THE BEAUTY

Inside the cocoon, there is disintegration before development. Sometimes God allows situations that dismantle your confidence in yourself so you can depend fully on Him.

2 Corinthians 12:9 says: **"My grace is sufficient for thee: for my strength is made perfect in weakness."**

Weakness is not failure. It is transformation territory. You may not recognize yourself in this season, but God is reshaping you.

PRAYER

Lord, if I must enter the cocoon, give me grace to remain. Help me not to fight hidden seasons. Remove pride. Remove self-reliance. Break what needs breaking. Dissolve what cannot go into my next level. Even when I feel unseen, let me rest in knowing You see me. I trust You in the dark. In Jesus' name. Amen.

PROPHETIC DECLARATION

I declare that my hidden season is holy. God is reconstructing me from the inside out. What feels like breaking is becoming. I am not forgotten. I am being formed.

Chapter 6

When God Wraps You in Silence

The cocoon is silent. There is no visible movement. No outward sign of progress. Silence can be unsettling. We equate noise with growth. We equate activity with productivity. But silence is often where God speaks loudest.

SILENCE IS NOT ABSENCE

Psalm 46:10 says: **"Be still, and know that I am God."**

Stillness builds intimacy. When God wraps you in silence, He is removing distractions.

Hosea 2:14 says: **"I will allure her, and bring her into the wilderness, and speak comfortably unto her."**

God often speaks in wilderness seasons. Elijah heard God not in the wind, earthquake, or fire but in a still small voice (**see 1 Kings 19:12**). Silence refines your hearing.

INCUBATION REQUIRES ISOLATION

In silence:

- Character deepens.
- Motives are purified.
- Identity stabilizes.

Galatians 6:9 reminds us: **"Let us not be weary in well doing: for in due season we shall reap, if we faint not."**

Due season requires waiting.

Isaiah 40:31 says: **"They that wait upon the Lord shall renew their strength."**

Waiting renews. Waiting stretches. Waiting strengthens. Inside silence, your spiritual muscles are forming.

WHEN HEAVEN FEELS QUIET

There are moments when prayers seem unanswered. But silence does not mean rejection. Daniel prayed for 21 days before a breakthrough came (**see Daniel 10**).

Behind the scenes, heaven was working. Just because you cannot see movement does not mean God is inactive.

Psalm 121:4 assures us: **"He that keepeth Israel shall neither slumber nor sleep."**

Even in your quietest season, God is working.

PRAYER

Father, teach me to trust You in quiet seasons. When I do not hear immediate answers, anchor me in faith. Remove anxiety that comes from waiting. Let silence refine my character and deepen my trust. Help me to believe that You are working, even when I cannot see it. I surrender to Your timing. In Jesus' name. Amen.

PROPHETIC DECLARATION

I declare that silence will not shake my faith. God is working behind the scenes. My waiting is not wasted. My stillness is strengthening me. When I emerge, I will emerge stronger.

Chapter 7

The Crushing, The Breaking, The Dissolving

Inside the cocoon, something radical happens. The caterpillar does not slowly grow wings. It dissolves. Its former structure breaks down into what scientists describe as a cellular "soup." The body that once crawled disintegrates before the butterfly forms. It is not improvement. It is reconstruction. And spiritually, this is the stage most believers misunderstand.

GOD DOES NOT ALWAYS IMPROVE YOU, HE REBUILDS YOU

We often pray, *"Lord, fix me."* But sometimes God answers, *"I must break you before I build you."*

Jeremiah 18:4 says: **"And the vessel that he made of clay was marred in the hand of the potter: so he made it again another vessel, as seemed good to the potter to make it."**

Notice: **He made it again.** There are seasons when God dismantles former versions of you. Not because He is angry. But because He is intentional.

Isaiah 64:8 declares: **"But now, O Lord, thou art our father; we are the clay, and thou our potter; and we all are the work of thy hand."**

The clay does not dictate the shaping; the potter does.

THE CRUSHING PRODUCES OIL

Olives are crushed to release oil. Grapes are pressed to produce wine. Seeds break open before they sprout.

Psalm 34:18 says: **"The Lord is nigh unto them that are of a broken heart."**

Brokenness is not rejection; it is positioning. There are seasons when God allows disappointments, betrayals, closed doors, misunderstandings and isolation, and it feels like you are dissolving. But what if this dissolution is divine?

2 Corinthians 4:16 says: **"Though our outward man perish, yet the inward man is renewed day by day."**

While something is breaking externally, something is strengthening internally.

IDENTITY DISRUPTION BEFORE IDENTITY REVELATION

In the cocoon stage, the caterpillar loses its former identity completely. It cannot crawl anymore. But it cannot yet fly. It is in-between. Spiritually, this is the hardest place. You no longer fit your old environment. But you have not yet entered your new one.

Abraham experienced this. God called him out of his father's house (**see Genesis 12**), but the promise was not immediate.

Moses left Egypt but spent 40 years in Midian before leading Israel. Jesus was baptized in the Jordan before being led into the wilderness (**see Matthew 3–4**). The breaking always precedes the breakthrough.

THE FEAR OF LOSING YOURSELF

The crushing can make you question:

- Who am I now?
- Why is everything changing?
- Why does this hurt so deeply?
- Why do I feel dismantled?

But John 15:2 says: **"Every branch that beareth fruit, he purgeth it, that it may bring forth more fruit."**

Pruning is painful but it increases productivity. Sometimes God must strip away:

- False confidence
- Pride
- Over-dependence on people
- Insecure attachments
- Fear-based decisions

Because butterflies cannot carry caterpillar mindsets.

DO NOT RESIST THE DISSOLVING

If the caterpillar resisted the breakdown process, transformation would halt. Likewise, resistance to spiritual pruning delays elevation.

Hebrews 12:11 says: **"Now no chastening for the present seemeth to be joyous, but grievous: nevertheless afterward it yieldeth the peaceable fruit of righteousness…"**

Afterward. There is an afterward to your breaking. There is glory after this crushing.

Romans 8:18 assures us: **"For I reckon that the sufferings of this present time are not worthy to be compared with the glory which shall be revealed in us."**

Notice—revealed in us. Transformation is internal before it becomes visible.

PRAYER

Father, when You allow breaking, help me not to run. When You dismantle old structures, help me not to cling to them. If I must dissolve to become who You called me to be, give me the strength to surrender. Remove everything that cannot sustain my next level. Let the crushing produce oil. Let the breaking produce beauty. I trust Your hands, even when they press me. In Jesus' name. Amen.

PROPHETIC DECLARATION

I declare that my crushing is not my conclusion. God is reconstructing me for greater glory. What is breaking is making room for becoming. I will not resist divine rebuilding. My latter glory will be greater than my former.

Chapter 8

Trusting God When You Don't Recognize Yourself

There is a moment in transformation when the butterfly begins to form, but it does not yet look complete. Its wings are folded. Its colors are not fully visible. Its body is fragile. This is the in-between stage.

Spiritually, there comes a time when you look in the mirror and barely recognize yourself. You think differently. You respond differently. You desire differently. Old desires fade. Old reactions soften. Old ambitions shift. And it can feel unsettling.

THE DISCOMFORT OF GROWTH

Growth stretches identity.

2 Corinthians 3:18 says: **"But we all, with open face beholding as in a glass the glory of the Lord, are changed into the same image from glory to glory."**

From glory to glory. Change is progressive. You may feel:

- Emotionally sensitive
- Spiritually stretched
- Relationally disconnected
- Mentally challenged

But this is spiritual expansion.

Isaiah 43:18–19 says: **"Remember ye not the former things… Behold, I will do a new thing."**

New things feel unfamiliar.

OUTGROWING FORMER VERSIONS OF YOURSELF

Butterflies cannot return to being caterpillars. When transformation begins, you will outgrow:

- Conversations that once entertained you.
- Environments that once felt comfortable.
- Relationships rooted in dysfunction.
- Habits tied to insecurity.

Philippians 3:13 says: **"Forgetting those things which are behind, and reaching forth unto those things which are before."**

Reaching forward requires releasing backward.

WHEN OTHERS DON'T RECOGNIZE YOU EITHER

Transformation can make people uncomfortable. The people who knew you in your crawling stage may struggle with your wings.

David's own brothers underestimated him. Joseph's brothers rejected him. Paul's past made believers doubt him initially. But Galatians 1:10 says: **"For do I now persuade men, or God?"** You cannot evolve and seek universal approval. Trust God's approval.

IDENTITY ROOTED IN CHRIST

Your identity must shift from performance to purpose.

Colossians 3:3 says: **"For ye are dead, and your life is hid with Christ in God."**

Hidden identity produces secure transformation. You may not recognize yourself, but God does. He sees the butterfly forming inside the cocoon.

PRAYER

Lord, as I change, anchor me in You. When I do not recognize myself, remind me that You are shaping me. Remove fear of growth. Remove insecurity tied to past identity. Help me to embrace the new version You are forming. Let my identity be rooted in Christ alone. In Jesus' name. Amen.

PROPHETIC DECLARATION

I declare that I am evolving by divine design. I will not cling to outdated versions of myself. God is shifting my identity for greater impact. I embrace the new thing He is doing in me. My transformation is permanent.

Chapter 9

The Danger of Leaving the Cocoon Too Soon

One of the most dangerous things you can do is rush transformation. If someone cuts open a cocoon to "help" a butterfly emerge, the butterfly dies. Why? Because the struggle pushes fluid into the wings. Without struggle, there is no strength.

PREMATURE EXPOSURE IS DANGEROUS

Ecclesiastes 3:11 says: **"He hath made every thing beautiful in his time."**

In His time. Premature promotion can damage unprepared character. David was anointed king years before he wore the crown. Joseph had dreams long before the palace. Even Jesus waited until age thirty to begin ministry. Timing protects destiny.

STRUGGLE STRENGTHENS CAPACITY

The pushing, the resistance, the stretching—it builds strength.

James 1:4 reminds us: **"Let patience have her perfect work."**

If patience does not finish its work, weakness remains. Many people abort the process because the discomfort feels unbearable. But discomfort is developing capacity.

TRUST THE TIMING OF EMERGENCE

Psalm 31:15 says: **"My times are in thy hand."**

Not in public opinion. Not in comparison. Not in pressure. In God's hand. When it is time, you will emerge strong enough to sustain your altitude.

PRAYER

Father, deliver me from rushing what You are building. Help me to remain in process until strength is complete. Remove impatience. Remove comparison. Teach me to trust divine timing. Let my wings be fully formed before I fly. In Jesus' name. Amen.

PROPHETIC DECLARATION

I declare that I will not rush God's process. My timing is in His hands. My struggle is strengthening me. I will emerge complete, prepared, and powerful. Nothing premature will sabotage my destiny.

Part III

Strength During Process

Chapter 10

Emerging with New Wings

There comes a moment when the struggle inside the cocoon reaches completion. The butterfly pushes. The casing cracks. Light enters. And what once crawled now steps into air. Emergence is not loud; it is sacred. It is the visible evidence of invisible obedience.

EMERGENCE FOLLOWS ENDURANCE

Galatians 6:9 declares: **"And let us not be weary in well doing: for in due season we shall reap, if we faint not."**

Due season is not accidental; it is earned through endurance. The butterfly does not emerge the day it enters the cocoon. It emerges when transformation is complete. Likewise, God does not release you when you are excited. He releases you when you are ready.

Psalm 105:19 says concerning Joseph: **"Until the time that his word came: the word of the Lord tried him."**

The Word tests before it manifests.

NEW WINGS REQUIRE NEW BALANCE

When the butterfly first emerges, its wings are wet and fragile. It must remain still for a moment. The fluid pumped through struggle must settle. Spiritually, after breakthrough comes stability. Many people sabotage emergence because they rush the first flight. When God elevates you:

- Stay humble.
- Stay grounded in prayer.
- Stay submitted.
- Stay disciplined.

Proverbs 4:18 says: **"But the path of the just is as the shining light, that shineth more and more unto the perfect day."**

Growth continues, even after emergence.

YOU CANNOT FLY WITH A CRAWLING MENTALITY

Emergence changes perspective. The caterpillar saw leaves. The butterfly sees landscapes.

Isaiah 55:8–9 reminds us: **"For my thoughts are not your thoughts... For as the heavens are higher than the earth, so are my ways higher than your ways."**

God elevates your thinking before He elevates your position. New wings demand:

- New boundaries
- New discernment

- New prayer depth
- New spiritual authority

Colossians 3:2 says: **"Set your affection on things above, not on things on the earth."**

Your altitude changes your focus.

THE RESPONSIBILITY OF FLIGHT

Emergence is not just freedom; it is responsibility.

Luke 12:48 says: **"For unto whomsoever much is given, of him shall be much required."**

Wings are not decorative. They are functional. You were not transformed merely to admire yourself. You were transformed to fulfill purpose.

PRAYER

Father, as I emerge into new dimensions, keep my heart pure. Let humility guard my elevation. Help me to steward the wings You have given me. Protect me from pride and distraction. Teach me to fly in obedience and not in ego. Let my emergence glorify You alone. In Jesus' name. Amen.

PROPHETIC DECLARATION

I declare that my season of emergence has come. My endurance has produced readiness. My wings are strong and prepared. I will not return to crawling. I will soar in humility and authority.

Chapter 11

You Cannot Go Back to the Leaf

One of the greatest temptations after transformation is familiarity. The butterfly cannot return to being a caterpillar, but sometimes believers try. After breakthrough, they revisit:

- Old relationships
- Old thought patterns
- Old insecurities
- Old environments

But flight changes compatibility.

ELEVATION CHANGES ACCESS

Genesis 19 records Lot's wife looking back. Looking back cost her forward movement.

Philippians 3:13–14 says: **"Forgetting those things which are behind… I press toward the mark."**

Pressing requires forward focus. You cannot carry old leaves into new skies. Some environments were only meant for your crawling season. When God elevates you, some spaces become too small.

THE COMFORT OF THE FAMILIAR

Caterpillars are comfortable on leaves. Flight requires courage. Exodus 16 shows Israel longing for Egypt, even after deliverance. Bondage can feel familiar, but familiarity is not destiny.

Isaiah 43:18 says: **"Remember ye not the former things."**

Do not romanticize what God rescued you from.

GROWTH REQUIRES SEPARATION

2 Corinthians 6:17 declares: **"Come out from among them, and be ye separate."**

Separation is not arrogance; it is alignment. Butterflies feed differently. They move differently. They see differently. You cannot shrink to fit people who are uncomfortable with your wings.

Proverbs 18:1 warns against isolation for selfish reasons, but divine separation for destiny is different. Jesus often withdrew to pray (**see Luke 5:16**). Separation strengthens clarity.

HONOR THE PROCESS BY PROTECTING THE OUTCOME

If you dishonor the process, you jeopardize the promise.

Galatians 5:1 says: **"Stand fast therefore in the liberty wherewith Christ hath made us free."**

Do not entangle yourself again. You did not endure crushing to return to crawling.

PRAYER

Lord, give me the courage to let go of what no longer aligns with my growth. Deliver me from nostalgia that sabotages destiny. Help me to honor my transformation by protecting it. Strengthen me to walk away from what diminishes my calling. Let me embrace the new fully. In Jesus' name. Amen.

PROPHETIC DECLARATION

I declare that I will not return to former limitations. I release the leaf. I release the past. I release outdated environments. My wings are too valuable to waste.

Chapter 12

From Survival to Soaring

The caterpillar survives. The butterfly soars. There is a difference between surviving and thriving. Survival mode focuses on:

- Avoiding harm
- Minimizing risk
- Staying safe

Soaring focuses on:

- Purpose
- Impact
- Vision
- Expansion

Many believers remain in survival, even after transformation. But God did not design you to merely endure life.

YOU WERE BUILT FOR ALTITUDE

Isaiah 40:31 declares: **"They that wait upon the Lord shall renew their strength; they shall mount up with wings as eagles."**

Mount up. Flight is spiritual elevation.

Psalm 18:33 says: **"He maketh my feet like hinds' feet, and setteth me upon my high places."**

High places represent authority and dominion. **Genesis 1:26** reminds us that humanity was given dominion. Dominion is not survival; it is stewardship.

LIVING ABOVE FEAR

Survival is fear-based. Soaring is faith-based.

2 Timothy 1:7 says: **"For God hath not given us the spirit of fear; but of power, and of love, and of a sound mind."**

Fear keeps you crawling. Faith lifts you higher. **Hebrews 11:1** defines faith as substance and evidence. Faith allows you to move, even when wind resistance increases.

THE PURPOSE OF ALTITUDE

Butterflies pollinate as they fly. Your soaring blesses others.

Matthew 5:16 says: **"Let your light so shine before men."**

Your transformation was not just personal; it was missional. When you soar:

- Others see possibility.
- Others gain hope.
- Others witness God's faithfulness.

SUSTAINING FLIGHT

Soaring requires:

- Continual prayer (**see 1 Thessalonians 5:17**)
- Renewed mind (**see Romans 12:2**)
- Ongoing humility (**see James 4:6**)
- Consistent obedience (**see Deuteronomy 28:1**)

Flight is sustained by relationship with God.

PRAYER

Father, deliver me from survival mentality. Teach me to soar in faith. Let fear lose its grip on my destiny. Give me the courage to move in purpose. Help me to use my elevation to bless others. Let my life reflect Your glory at every altitude. In Jesus' name. Amen.

PROPHETIC DECLARATION

I declare that I am moving from survival to soaring. Fear will not ground me. Faith will elevate me. My life will reflect God's glory. I was created for altitude.

Chapter 13

The Butterfly Effect – Your Transformation Blesses Others

A butterfly never flies without consequence. Every movement from flower to flower spreads pollen. Every landing leaves invisible impact. Every flight contributes to growth far beyond itself.

The butterfly does not strive to create change. It simply becomes what it was designed to be, and impact follows. So it is with you.

YOUR PROCESS WAS NEVER PRIVATE

You may have thought the crawling was personal. You may have thought the cocoon was isolated. You may have thought the crushing was individual. But heaven knew your transformation would be generational.

Genesis 50:20 — Joseph declares: **"Ye thought evil against me; but God meant it unto good, to save much people alive."**

Joseph's pit preserved a nation. Your process is preserving someone else's hope. What you endured in silence will become someone else's survival map.

TESTIMONY IS THE EVIDENCE OF PROCESS

Revelation 12:11 says: **"And they overcame him by the blood of the Lamb, and by the word of their testimony."**

Testimony is proof that transformation works. When people see you:

- Still standing after betrayal
- Still worshiping after loss
- Still faithful after disappointment
- Still serving after rejection

They gain permission to believe again. You are living evidence that the cocoon does not kill you; it refines you.

THE LEADERSHIP RESPONSIBILITY OF THE TRANSFORMED

In Luke 22:32, Jesus told Peter: **"When thou art converted, strengthen thy brethren."**

Notice the sequence: *Conversion → Strengthening Others.* Transformation carries responsibility. If you have wings, you are called to lift.

Galatians 6:2 says: **"Bear ye one another's burdens, and so fulfil the law of Christ."**

The church does not need perfect leaders; it needs processed leaders. Leaders who understand:

- Delay
- Hidden seasons
- Humility
- Dependence on God

Because leaders who skipped the process cannot shepherd the process.

A CHURCH THAT UNDERSTANDS PROCESS

When a church culture understands divine timing:

- It stops competing.
- It stops comparing.
- It stops forcing premature promotion.
- It starts cultivating character.

Ecclesiastes 3:1 declares: **"To every thing there is a season."**

Healthy churches honor seasons. Some are crawling. Some are cocooning. Some are emerging. Some are soaring, but all are necessary. **1 Corinthians 12:18** reminds us that God sets members in the body as it pleases Him. Your transformation strengthens the entire body.

GENERATIONAL IMPACT

Psalm 145:4 declares: **"One generation shall praise thy works to another."**

When you trust process, your children see faith. When you endure crushing, your spiritual sons and daughters inherit resilience. The butterfly effect is generational. Your obedience is multiplying beyond your awareness.

PRAYER

Father, let my transformation strengthen others. Keep pride far from me. Help me remember my crawling season, so I never judge someone else's. Use my testimony to restore faith. Let my wings pollinate purpose in others. May my life multiply hope across generations. In Jesus' name. Amen.

PROPHETIC DECLARATION

I declare that my transformation is generational. My obedience is multiplying impact. My endurance will strengthen leaders. My testimony will rescue the weary. I am not transformed for myself alone.

Chapter 14

Trust the Process – God Knows What He Is Doing

There is a sacred maturity that comes when you no longer demand explanations from God. You simply trust.

Proverbs 3:5–6 commands: **"Trust in the Lord with all thine heart; and lean not unto thine own understanding."**

Trust is not passive; it is surrender.

WHEN UNDERSTANDING FAILS

Habakkuk questioned God. Job questioned suffering. David questioned delay. Yet all learned that God's sovereignty surpasses human reasoning.

Isaiah 55:8 says: **"For my thoughts are not your thoughts."**

You may not understand:

- Why the door closed.
- Why the relationship ended.

- Why the silence lasted.
- Why the delay stretched.

But divine wisdom is never accidental.

Romans 11:33 declares: **"O the depth of the riches both of the wisdom and knowledge of God!"**

God sees what you cannot.

THE ARCHITECTURE OF DIVINE TIMING

Habakkuk 2:3 says: **"For the vision is yet for an appointed time."**

Appointed means scheduled. God is not improvising your life.

Psalm 37:23 says: **"The steps of a good man are ordered by the Lord."**

Ordered steps include:

- Detours
- Waiting rooms
- Wilderness seasons
- Hidden preparation

Nothing is wasted.

TRUSTING THROUGH PAIN

Romans 8:28 assures us that all things work together for good. All things include:

- Rejection
- Disappointment
- Delay
- Correction
- Pruning

Hebrews 12:11 reminds us that discipline produces righteousness afterward. Afterward is proof that pain is purposeful.

LEADERS MUST MODEL TRUST

Pastors, ministers, and leaders must embody trust publicly. If leaders panic in process, congregations lose confidence.

Psalm 125:1 says: **"They that trust in the Lord shall be as mount Zion, which cannot be removed."**

Mount Zion is stable. The church needs stable leaders. Trust anchors leadership.

PRAYER

Lord, even when my understanding fails, anchor me in trust. Let faith outgrow fear. Help me lead with stability. Teach me to rest in Your sovereignty. I surrender the need for explanations. I embrace confidence in Your wisdom. In Jesus' name. Amen.

PROPHETIC DECLARATION

I declare that my trust is unshakable. God is sovereign over my seasons. Nothing in my life is accidental. My steps are ordered. My future is secure in His hands.

Part IV

Emergence and Elevation

Chapter 15

Having Patience During the Process

Patience is one of the most difficult disciplines in spiritual growth. We do not struggle with faith when things are moving. We struggle with faith when things are waiting.

The caterpillar does not become a butterfly overnight. The cocoon stage is not rushed. There is no shortcut in metamorphosis. The transformation unfolds at the pace designed by its Creator. And so it is with you.

PATIENCE IS PROOF OF TRUST

Proverbs 3:5 declares: **"Trust in the Lord with all thine heart; and lean not unto thine own understanding."**

Patience is trust stretched over time. Anyone can trust God for a moment. Mature believers trust Him for a season. Waiting reveals what we truly believe about God. If we believe He is faithful, we wait differently. If we believe He is intentional, we wait peacefully. If we believe He is sovereign, we wait confidently. But if we doubt His goodness, impatience begins to dominate.

Psalm 27:14 instructs us: **"Wait on the Lord: be of good courage, and he shall strengthen thine heart."**

Waiting strengthens. Impatience weakens.

THE TENSION OF DELAYED RESULTS

One of the greatest battles during the process is delayed visibility. You pray, but there is no immediate answer. You serve, but there is no recognition. You obey, but there is no reward. And the flesh begins to whisper: *"Maybe this is not working."*

But Hebrews 10:36 reminds us: **"For ye have need of patience, that, after ye have done the will of God, ye might receive the promise."**

After. Patience bridges obedience and promise. The caterpillar cannot demand wings on day two. The cocoon cannot be forced open prematurely.

Ecclesiastes 3:11 declares: **"He hath made every thing beautiful in his time."**

In His time. Divine timing protects divine purpose.

PATIENCE DEVELOPS DEPTH

James 1:3–4 says: **"Knowing this, that the trying of your faith worketh patience. But let patience have her perfect work, that ye may be perfect and entire, wanting nothing."**

Patience completes you. Without patience:

- Character remains shallow.
- Faith remains fragile.
- Obedience remains conditional.

But patience deepens spiritual roots. **Colossians 2:7** speaks of being rooted and built up in Him. Roots form underground. Growth is often invisible before it becomes undeniable.

THE DANGER OF IMPATIENCE

Impatience tempts us to:

- Force doors open.
- Return to old environments.
- Accept lesser options.
- Abandon process entirely.

Abraham and Sarah grew impatient and produced Ishmael (**see Genesis 16**). The promise was delayed, but impatience complicated destiny. When we move ahead of God, we create avoidable battles.

Psalm 37:7 says: **"Rest in the Lord, and wait patiently for him."**

Rest and wait. Patience is not passive frustration; it is active trust.

WAITING IS NOT WASTING

Isaiah 40:31 declares: **"But they that wait upon the Lord shall renew their strength."**

Waiting renews strength. Notice—it does not drain it. The Hebrew understanding of "wait" implies expectancy, like twisting strands together to create strength.

While you wait:

- God is aligning details.
- God is strengthening capacity.
- God is preparing you for what you prayed for.

The cocoon looks inactive. But internally, transformation is accelerating. What feels slow externally may be intense internally.

PATIENCE IN LEADERSHIP

Leaders must especially cultivate patience. Ministry growth takes time. Spiritual maturity takes time. Character formation takes time. **1 Timothy 5:22** warns against laying hands suddenly on any man. Premature promotion damages people. Healthy leaders honor process in themselves and others.

Galatians 6:9 says: **"Let us not be weary in well doing."**

Weariness tempts us to rush, but patience produces stability.

THE EMOTIONAL BATTLE OF WAITING

Patience does not mean you will not feel frustration. David often cried out in the Psalms: **"How long, O Lord?" (Psalm 13:1).** Yet he always returned to trust. You may feel:

- Overlooked.
- Forgotten.
- Overqualified for your current season.
- Ready before release.

But readiness in your eyes is not always readiness in God's design. **Habakkuk 2:3** reminds us that vision has an appointed time. Appointed means scheduled. God is not improvising your future.

DEVELOPING A PATIENT SPIRIT

How do we cultivate patience during process?

1. Stay rooted in the Word.

Psalm 119:105 — His Word guides perspective.

2. Maintain prayer discipline.

Philippians 4:6 — Bring anxiety to God.

3. Resist comparison.

Galatians 6:4 — Examine your own work.

4. Remember past faithfulness.

Psalm 77:11 — Recall what God has done.

5. Practice gratitude in waiting.

1 Thessalonians 5:18 — Give thanks in everything. Gratitude stabilizes impatience.

WHEN PATIENCE PRODUCES PROMOTION

1 Peter 5:6 declares: **"Humble yourselves therefore under the mighty hand of God, that he may exalt you in due time."**

Due time. Exaltation that comes too early collapses, but elevation that follows patience endures. The butterfly emerges when the struggle has strengthened its wings.

When you finally step into your next season, you will recognize:

- The waiting was building endurance.
- The delay was building discipline.
- The silence was building sensitivity to God's voice.

ENCOURAGEMENT

If you are tired of waiting, hear this: *Your patience is not unnoticed.* **Hebrews 6:12** speaks of those who, through faith and patience, inherit the promises. *Faith and patience.* Not faith alone. Not patience alone. Both together produce inheritance. You are not behind schedule. You are on divine timing.

PRAYER

Father, teach me to wait without anxiety. Strengthen me to trust without timelines. Remove comparison from my heart. Guard me from rushing what You are building. Help me to remain faithful in unseen seasons. Let patience complete its work in me. I surrender my timing to Yours. In Jesus' name. Amen.

PROPHETIC DECLARATION

I declare that I will not rush God's process. I will not compare my season to another's. My waiting is strengthening me. My patience is producing maturity. My promise is protected by divine timing. I will wait, and I will emerge ready.

Chapter 16

How to Remain Strong While Hidden

There is a strength that is formed in public. And then there is a strength that is formed in private. Public strength is visible. Private strength is developed.

Hidden seasons are often the most misunderstood stages of spiritual growth. When visibility decreases, many assume significance has diminished. When applause fades, many assume purpose has stalled. But heaven measures differently. God does His deepest work where no one claps.

HIDDEN DOES NOT MEAN FORGOTTEN

One of the greatest lies during hidden seasons is this: *"God has forgotten me."*

Isaiah 49:15–16 declares: **"Can a woman forget her sucking child…? Yea, they may forget, yet will I not forget thee. Behold, I have graven thee upon the palms of my hands."**

Hidden does not mean erased. Joseph was hidden in prison, but heaven was aligning a palace. David was hidden in fields, but heaven was preparing a throne. Moses was hidden in Midian, but heaven was preparing a deliverer.

Psalm 31:15 says: **"My times are in thy hand."**

Not in public opinion. Not in social validation. Not in human timelines. In His hand.

THE STRENGTH OF OBSCURITY

Obscurity builds spiritual muscle. When no one is watching:

- Your motives are purified.
- Your discipline is tested.
- Your character is exposed.
- Your dependency on God increases.

Matthew 6:6 says: **"But thou, when thou prayest, enter into thy closet… and thy Father which seeth in secret shall reward thee openly."**

Secret faithfulness precedes open reward. If you cannot be strong without recognition, visibility will weaken you. Hidden seasons protect you from premature exposure.

DEEPENING ROOTS UNDERGROUND

Colossians 2:7 speaks of being **"rooted and built up in Him."** Roots grow underground. Before a tree rises high, it grows deep. The higher the calling, the deeper the roots required.

Psalm 92:12–13 says: **"The righteous shall flourish like the palm tree… Those that be planted in the house of the Lord shall flourish."**

Flourishing begins with planting. Planting is hidden. If you rush exposure before roots are secure, storms will uproot you.Hidden seasons are root seasons.

GUARDING YOUR HEART WHILE HIDDEN

Proverbs 4:23 warns: **"Keep thy heart with all diligence; for out of it are the issues of life."**

Hidden seasons can breed:

- Bitterness
- Comparison
- Insecurity
- Self-doubt
- Impatience

When you see others elevated while you remain unseen, the flesh whispers: *"Why not me?"* But Galatians 6:4 says: **"Let every man prove his own work, and then shall he have rejoicing in himself alone, and not in another."**

Comparison is the thief of peace in hidden seasons. Your assignment is not identical to theirs. Your timing is not identical to theirs. Your preparation is not identical to theirs. Stay focused.

STRENGTH THROUGH INTIMACY

Hidden seasons increase intimacy.

Hosea 2:14 says: **"I will allure her, and bring her into the wilderness, and speak comfortably unto her."**

God often speaks most clearly in isolation. In visibility, noise is loud. In hiddenness, His voice becomes clearer.

Psalm 46:10 declares: **"Be still, and know that I am God."**

Stillness builds knowing. The cocoon is quiet for a reason. God removes distractions to deepen relationship. If you use hidden seasons to cultivate intimacy, you will emerge with spiritual authority.

EMOTIONAL RESILIENCE IN ISOLATION

Even strong believers struggle emotionally while hidden. David cried, **"How long, O Lord?" (Psalm 13:1).** Elijah felt alone. Jeremiah felt rejected. Paul endured imprisonment. But none allowed hidden seasons to cancel obedience.

2 Corinthians 4:8–9 reminds us: **"We are troubled on every side, yet not distressed… cast down, but not destroyed."**

Hidden seasons test emotional stability. To remain strong:

- Stay consistent in prayer.
- Stay grounded in scripture.
- Stay accountable to wise counsel.
- Stay grateful even in small victories.
-

Gratitude stabilizes discouragement.

RESIST THE URGE TO SELF-PROMOTE

One of the greatest temptations while hidden is self-promotion. When doors do not open quickly, the flesh wants to force them. But Psalm 75:6–7 declares: **"For promotion cometh neither from the east, nor from the west… But God is the judge: he putteth down one, and setteth up another."**

If God elevates you, no one can stop it. If you elevate yourself, sustainability becomes fragile. Jesus Himself waited thirty years before public ministry. If the Son of God honored process, so must we.

STRENGTH COMES FROM IDENTITY, NOT VISIBILITY

Colossians 3:3 says: **"For ye are dead, and your life is hid with Christ in God."**

Your identity is secure, even when your platform is small. You are not valuable because you are seen. You are valuable because you are called. Hidden seasons refine identity so that when visibility comes, ego does not dominate.

HIDDEN BUT NOT IDLE

Being hidden does not mean being inactive. While hidden:

- Develop your gift.
- Sharpen your skills.
- Study deeply.
- Pray consistently.
- Serve faithfully.

Luke 16:10 reminds us: **"He that is faithful in that which is least is faithful also in much."**

Hidden faithfulness qualifies you for visible responsibility.

TRUSTING GOD'S TIMING COMPLETELY

Habakkuk 2:3 says: **"Though it tarry, wait for it."**

Tarry does not mean denial; it means development. The cocoon stage may feel long, but emergence always comes when transformation is complete.

Isaiah 60:22 declares: **"When the time is right, I, the Lord, will make it happen."**

When the time is right. Not early. Not late. *Right.*

ENCOURAGEMENT

If you are hidden right now:

- You are not stuck.
- You are being strengthened.
- You are not delayed.
- You are being developed.
- You are not overlooked.
- You are being overhauled internally.

Hidden seasons are holy. They shape leaders. They build endurance. They deepen faith. They strengthen conviction. They cultivate humility. And when you emerge, you will carry a depth that applause alone could never produce.

PRAYER

Father, strengthen me in hidden seasons. Guard my heart from comparison. Remove impatience from my spirit. Teach me to value private development over public recognition. Let my roots grow deep. Let my faith mature in silence. When the time comes for visibility, let me emerge grounded, humble, and prepared. In Jesus' name. Amen.

PROPHETIC DECLARATION

I declare that I will remain strong while hidden. My roots are growing deeper. My faith is becoming stronger. My character is being refined. God sees me in secret. When the time is right, He will elevate me. Until then, I will remain faithful.

Chapter 17

Overcoming Discouragement During the Process

Discouragement is one of the most dangerous emotions during process. It does not usually arrive loudly. It creeps in quietly and whispers when prayers feel unanswered. It grows when delays stretch longer than expected. It strengthens when comparison begins.

Discouragement is not always dramatic but if left unchecked, it can paralyze destiny. Many believers survive crushing seasons but struggle with discouragement in hidden seasons. The cocoon is not just dark; it is silent. And silence tests emotional endurance.

DISCOURAGEMENT IS A BATTLE OF PERSPECTIVE

Numbers 13 tells the story of the twelve spies. All saw the same land. All saw the same giants. But ten returned discouraged, while two—Joshua and Caleb—returned confident. The land did not change. Perspective did. Discouragement magnifies obstacles and minimizes promises. Faith magnifies promises and minimizes obstacles.

Psalm 42:5 records David speaking to his own soul: **"Why art thou cast down, O my soul? and why art thou disquieted in me? hope thou in God."**

Notice: David did not deny his discouragement. He confronted it. Sometimes overcoming discouragement begins by speaking truth to yourself.

RECOGNIZING THE SOURCE

Discouragement often comes from:

- Delayed expectations
- Unmet timelines
- Comparison
- Isolation
- Fatigue
- Repeated disappointment

Proverbs 13:12 says: **"Hope deferred maketh the heart sick."** Delayed hope can weaken emotional strength. But the verse continues: **"But when the desire cometh, it is a tree of life."** Delay is not denial; it is development.

THE EMOTIONAL WEIGHT OF WAITING

Even the strongest leaders faced discouragement. Elijah, after a powerful victory in 1 Kings 18, became discouraged in chapter 19. He sat under a tree and asked God to take his life. Exhaustion intensified his discouragement. Sometimes you are not spiritually weak; you are simply tired. God did not rebuke Elijah. He let him rest. He fed him. He restored him. Then He spoke again. Rest is sometimes the remedy for discouragement.

STRENGTHENING YOURSELF IN THE LORD

1 Samuel 30:6 says of David: **"But David encouraged himself in the Lord his God."**

When others could not encourage him, he strengthened himself. Encouragement is not always external. Sometimes it is intentional.

To overcome discouragement:

1. **Revisit what God has already done.**

Psalm 77:11 — **"I will remember the works of the Lord."**

2. **Reaffirm God's promises aloud.**

Faith grows when spoken (**see Romans 10:17**).

3. **Refuse comparison.**

Galatians 6:4 reminds us to examine our own work.

4. **Guard your thoughts.**

2 Corinthians 10:5 — bring every thought into captivity. Discouragement thrives in unchecked thinking.

THE TRAP OF COMPARISON

Discouragement often grows when you compare your process to someone else's outcome. You see others emerging while you remain hidden. You see others promoted while you are preparing.

But 2 Corinthians 10:12 warns that comparing ourselves among ourselves is not wise. You do not know their preparation. You do not know their timing. You do not know their struggles. Your assignment is to remain faithful in your lane.

WHEN PRAYERS SEEM UNANSWERED

Daniel prayed for 21 days before breakthrough came (**see Daniel 10**). Behind the scenes, spiritual warfare was unfolding. Just because you do not see movement does not mean heaven is inactive.

Isaiah 55:11 assures: **"So shall my word be… it shall not return unto me void."**

God's promises have momentum, even when progress feels invisible.

REFUSING TO QUIT

Galatians 6:9 declares: **"Let us not be weary in well doing: for in due season we shall reap, if we faint not."**

The condition is clear: *if we faint not.* Discouragement tempts you to faint before fulfillment. The enemy cannot stop your calling, but he will try to exhaust your endurance. But Isaiah 40:29 says: **"He giveth power to the faint; and to them that have no might he increaseth strength."** God strengthens the weary, not the self-sufficient.

EMOTIONAL HONESTY WITHOUT SPIRITUAL SURRENDER

It is possible to acknowledge discouragement without surrendering to it. Jesus in Gethsemane said: **"My soul is exceeding sorrowful." (Matthew 26:38).** He acknowledged sorrow, but He still obeyed. Emotions are real nut they are not rulers.

2 Corinthians 5:7 says: **"For we walk by faith, not by sight."**

Faith includes walking through emotional valleys.

WORSHIP BREAKS DISCOURAGEMENT

In Acts 16:25, Paul and Silas sang in prison. Worship shifts the atmosphere. Praise redirects focus. Discouragement shrinks in the presence of worship.

Psalm 34:1 declares: **"I will bless the Lord at all times: his praise shall continually be in my mouth."**

Praise during the process builds resilience.

THE STRENGTH THAT COMES AFTER

James 1:12 says: **"Blessed is the man that endureth temptation: for when he is tried, he shall receive the crown of life."**

After endurance comes reward. After struggle comes strength. After discouragement comes clarity. The butterfly struggles before flight, but the struggle strengthens the wings. Your discouragement is not permanent; your destiny is.

A WORD TO LEADERS

Pastors, ministers, and leaders often experience hidden discouragement. You encourage others while fighting silent battles. You preach faith while wrestling fatigue. But 1 Corinthians 15:58 reminds you: **"Be ye stedfast, unmoveable, always abounding in the work of the Lord."**

Your labor is not in vain. God sees unseen sacrifices. He records hidden tears. He honors persistent obedience.

ENCOURAGEMENT

If discouragement has visited you during this process: D*o not build it a home.* It may knock, but it does not have to stay. God is still working. Your process is still active. Your promise is still intact. The cocoon may feel long but wings are still forming.

PRAYER

Father, when discouragement whispers, strengthen my faith. Guard my thoughts. Renew my perspective. Help me to remember Your promises when delay feels heavy. Give me rest when I am weary. Give me courage when I feel faint. Let worship rise even in silence. I refuse to quit before fulfillment. In Jesus' name. Amen.

PROPHETIC DECLARATION

I declare that discouragement will not derail my destiny. My faith is stronger than my feelings. God is working behind the scenes. My due season is coming. I will not faint. I will emerge victorious.

Part V

Commissioning and Impact

Chapter 18

Be Careful Who You Allow in Your Process Season

Process seasons are fragile seasons. The cocoon is not a public space. It is sacred. It is vulnerable. It is protective. And not everyone should have access to you while you are becoming.

The caterpillar does not invite observers into the chrysalis. The transformation happens in guarded isolation because exposure during development can damage formation. Likewise, you must guard your process.

NOT EVERYONE CAN HANDLE YOUR BECOMING

When you are in a growth season:

- Your identity is shifting.
- Your emotions may be tender.
- Your discernment is sharpening.
- Your spiritual capacity is stretching.

You are not weak; you are developing. But development requires protection.

Proverbs 4:23 says: **"Keep thy heart with all diligence; for out of it are the issues of life."**

Your heart is especially sensitive during the process. If you allow negative voices into your cocoon season, they can disrupt your confidence. Some people are comfortable with your crawling stage but uncomfortable with your wings.

THE DANGER OF PREMATURE EXPOSURE

If someone cuts open a cocoon to "help" the butterfly, it dies because the struggle strengthens the wings. In the same way, some people will try to "rescue" you from necessary stretching:

- They will tell you to quit.
- They will tell you you're doing too much.
- They will discourage your growth.
- They will minimize your calling.

But Galatians 1:10 asks: **"For do I now persuade men, or God?"** Your process is not a group project; it is a divine appointment.

GUARDING YOUR VISION

When God is shaping you, your vision may still be forming. If you share it too early with the wrong people, they may:

- Dismiss it.
- Mock it.
- Misinterpret it.
- Compete with it.

Joseph shared his dreams prematurely in Genesis 37, and jealousy followed. Not every vision is meant for every ear. Ecclesiastes 3:7 says there is: **"A time to keep silence, and a time to speak."** Wisdom knows the difference.

DISCERNMENT IN RELATIONSHIPS

During process seasons, ask yourself:

- Does this person push me toward God or away from discipline?
- Do they respect my growth?
- Do they honor my boundaries?
- Do they speak life or sow doubt?

1 Corinthians 15:33 warns: **"Evil communications corrupt good manners."**

Not everyone is evil, but some are immature, and immaturity can still sabotage development. Choose voices that:

- Strengthen your faith.
- Challenge your character.
- Encourage your obedience.
- Protect your integrity.

SOME PEOPLE ARE ASSIGNED TO A SEASON, NOT A LIFETIME

Ecclesiastes 3:1 reminds us that there is a season for everything. Some relationships are seasonal. They were necessary in your crawling stage. But they may not survive your flying stage. That does not make them bad. It makes them timed. As you grow, compatibility shifts.

2 Corinthians 6:17 says: **"Come out from among them, and be ye separate."**

Separation is not arrogance; it is alignment.

BE CAREFUL OF ENERGY DRAINERS

Process seasons require emotional energy. You cannot afford constant drama. You cannot afford constant negativity. You cannot afford constant distraction.

Nehemiah 6:3 says: **"I am doing a great work, so that I cannot come down."**

When you are building internally, you cannot descend into unnecessary conflict. Protect your focus. Protect your peace. Protect your prayer life.

THE ROLE OF WISE COUNSEL

Guarding your process does not mean isolation from everyone; it means intentional access.

Proverbs 11:14 says: **"In the multitude of counsellors there is safety."**

Choose mature, spiritually grounded voices. Choose mentors who have endured their own cocoon seasons. Choose accountability that strengthens discipline.

Jesus had twelve disciples but only three entered deeper moments like the Mount of Transfiguration (**see Matthew 17**). Access is layered. Not everyone receives equal access.

WHEN FAMILIARITY BECOMES LIMITATION

Some people are attached to your former version. They expect you to react the same way. They expect you to stay small. They expect you to stay accessible in ways that compromise growth. But **2 Corinthians 5:17** reminds us that you are a new creature. New creatures require new boundaries. If someone only values your old identity, they may resist your transformation. Do not shrink to maintain comfort.

LEADERSHIP WARNING

Pastors and leaders must be especially careful. Not everyone celebrating you is safe. Not everyone criticizing you is wrong. Discernment matters. **1 Peter 5:8** warns us to be sober and vigilant. Spiritual growth attracts both support and opposition. Guard your inner circle. Guard confidential struggles. Guard strategic decisions. The cocoon is sacred.

ASK THESE QUESTIONS

Before allowing someone close during the process, ask:

1. Do they honor confidentiality?
2. Do they respect boundaries?
3. Do they pray for me or pry into me?
4. Do they celebrate growth or compete with it?
5. Do they challenge me in love?

If the answer is no, limit access. Not in bitterness but in wisdom.

PROTECTING PEACE

Philippians 4:7 promises: **"The peace of God… shall keep your hearts and minds through Christ Jesus."**

Peace guards your mind during transformation. You cannot allow constant emotional turbulence. Your peace is fuel for your process. Guard it.

ENCOURAGEMENT

Your process season is sacred. Do not allow:

- Doubt-filled voices.
- Jealous hearts.
- Immature opinions.
- Competitive spirits.
- Fear-based counsel.

These will disrupt what God is shaping. The cocoon must remain intact until the wings are ready. You do not owe everyone access to your becoming. You owe God obedience.

PRAYER

Father, give me discernment in my relationships. Help me to recognize who is assigned to strengthen me and who may hinder me. Guard my heart during this season. Remove unhealthy attachments. Surround me with wise counsel. Teach me to protect what You are forming in me. Let my boundaries honor Your purpose. In Jesus' name. Amen.

PROPHETIC DECLARATION

I declare that my process is protected. God is guarding my development. I will not allow unhealthy voices into sacred seasons. My boundaries are aligned with my destiny. Only those assigned by God will have access to my becoming. My wings are forming and they will not be sabotaged.

Chapter 19

When People Misunderstand Your Growth

Growth is beautiful, but it is not always understood. When you begin to change—spiritually, emotionally, mentally—not everyone will celebrate it. Some will question it. Some will misinterpret it. Some will feel threatened by it. Others will resist it.

The caterpillar's transformation into a butterfly is natural but if another caterpillar could observe it, it might not understand what is happening.

- *"Why are you isolating?"*
- *"Why are you changing?"*
- *"Why don't you react the same way anymore?"*

Growth shifts patterns, and pattern-shifts can confuse people who are comfortable with your former version.

NOT EVERYONE RECOGNIZES THE NEW YOU

2 Corinthians 5:17 declares: **"If any man be in Christ, he is a new creature: old things are passed away; behold, all things are become new."**

New creatures do not behave like old ones. You may now:

- Walk away from arguments you once entertained.
- Decline invitations you once embraced.
- Refuse environments you once tolerated.
- Set boundaries you once ignored.

And when you do, some will say: *"You've changed."* Yes. That is the point. Growth requires change.

FAMILIARITY STRUGGLES WITH EVOLUTION

The people who knew you in your crawling stage may struggle with your wings. They were comfortable when you were:

- Accessible at all times.
- Easily influenced.
- Emotionally reactive.
- Less disciplined.
- Less focused.

But now, you are maturing.

Luke 2:52 says: **"And Jesus increased in wisdom and stature, and in favour with God and man."**

Even Jesus grew. Growth is biblical. But familiarity often resists elevation.

WHEN GROWTH FEELS LIKE REJECTION TO OTHERS

Sometimes your growth feels like rejection to those who are not growing with you. When you say "no" more often…When you protect your peace…When you prioritize prayer over social activity…People may interpret your boundaries as distance. But boundaries are not rejection. They are protection. **Proverbs 4:23** reminds us to guard our hearts.

If you do not guard growth, you will sabotage it to keep others comfortable.

JESUS WAS MISUNDERSTOOD

Mark 3:21 records that even Jesus' own family thought He was beside Himself.

John 6:66 says many disciples walked away when His teaching became difficult.

Growth attracts misunderstanding. If Jesus was misunderstood, we cannot expect universal approval.

Galatians 1:10 asks: **"For do I now persuade men, or God?"**

Your allegiance must remain with God, not with public opinion.

DO NOT REGRESS TO BE ACCEPTED

One of the greatest temptations when misunderstood is regression. You may feel pressure to:

- Laugh at jokes that dishonor your convictions.
- Rejoin conversations you outgrew.
- Re-enter environments that weaken you.
- Diminish your growth to avoid criticism.

But **Hebrews 10:38** warns against drawing back. You did not endure the process to retreat from progress. The butterfly cannot return to crawling without dying to its design.

EMOTIONAL PAIN OF BEING MISUNDERSTOOD

Let us be honest. It hurts. It hurts when long-time friends question you. It hurts when family misinterprets your growth. It hurts when colleagues mock your discipline. David felt this deeply. In Psalm 69:8 he said: **"I am become a stranger unto my brethren."** Growth can feel isolating, but isolation does not mean error. It often means elevation.

KEEP GROWING ANYWAY

Philippians 3:13–14 says: **"Forgetting those things which are behind... I press toward the mark."**

Pressing means moving forward despite resistance. Some people misunderstand because:

- They are uncomfortable with change.
- They are convicted by your discipline.

- They are insecure about their stagnation.
- They cannot access the same growth yet.

Your responsibility is not to convince them; it is to continue obeying God.

LEADERSHIP AND MISUNDERSTANDING

Leaders are often misunderstood during growth seasons. When vision expands, some will not see it immediately. When strategy shifts, some will resist. Nehemiah faced opposition when rebuilding the walls. But Nehemiah 6:3 declares: **"I am doing a great work, so that I cannot come down."**

Do not descend into constant explanation. Not everyone is assigned to understand your next level. Some are assigned to observe it later.

GROWTH REQUIRES ENDURANCE

James 1:4 says: **"Let patience have her perfect work."**

Patience includes enduring misunderstanding without retaliation. Jesus did not defend Himself before every critic. Sometimes silence is maturity. Sometimes restraint is strength. **Proverbs 17:28** says even a fool is considered wise when silent. Your peace is more important than winning arguments.

PRAY FOR THOSE WHO MISUNDERSTAND YOU

Matthew 5:44 instructs: **"Pray for them which despitefully use you."**

Not everyone who misunderstands you is malicious. Some are simply limited in perspective. Pray that God expands their understanding, but do not shrink your obedience while waiting.

STAND FIRM IN IDENTITY

Colossians 3:2 says: **"Set your affection on things above."**

When your identity is anchored in Christ, misunderstanding does not destabilize you. You know who you are. You know who called you. You know why you are growing. That clarity silences insecurity.

ENCOURAGEMENT

If people misunderstand your growth: *Keep growing.* If they question your boundaries: *Keep guarding your peace.* If they resist your maturity: *Keep developing.* If they misinterpret your distance: *Keep prioritizing obedience.* Time reveals transformation.

Eventually, fruit speaks louder than explanation. Matthew 7:16 reminds us: **"Ye shall know them by their fruits."** Let your fruit answer criticism. Let your consistency silence doubt. Let your humility sustain respect. You were not called to be universally understood. You were called to be obedient.

PRAYER

Father, when others misunderstand my growth, keep my heart pure. Remove bitterness. Remove defensiveness. Help me to grow without arrogance and mature without pride. Teach me to endure misunderstanding with grace. Let my fruit speak for itself. I choose obedience over approval. In Jesus' name. Amen.

PROPHETIC DECLARATION

I declare that misunderstanding will not stop my growth. I will not shrink to maintain comfort. I will not regress to regain approval. My identity is secure in Christ. My growth is ordained by God. I will continue becoming who He called me to be.

Chapter 20

A Final Charge – Trust God Completely

You have crawled. You have cocooned. You have been crushed. You have emerged. Now this is your charge. Trust God completely. Not partially. Not emotionally. Not seasonally. Completely.

A CHARGE TO INDIVIDUALS

Hebrews 10:35 says: **"Cast not away therefore your confidence."**

Do not lose confidence in the process. When new seasons come—and they will—trust again. Transformation is cyclical. Even butterflies lay eggs that begin new caterpillars. You will face future growth stages. Trust again.

A CHARGE TO LEADERS

To pastors and shepherds: Do not force people out of their cocoons. Do not compare spiritual growth speeds. Do not reward charisma over character. Develop patiently. **1 Peter 5:2–3** instructs leaders to shepherd willingly and by example. Be an example of trusting divine timing.

A CHARGE TO THE CHURCH

Church of the Living God: Return to patient discipleship. Return to character formation. Return to altar building. Return to prayerful waiting.

James 5:7 says: **"Be patient therefore, brethren, unto the coming of the Lord."**

The church must not rush what God is cultivating. Healthy transformation produces sustainable revival.

APOSTOLIC COMMISSION

I charge you:

- Trust when it is unclear.
- Stand when it is silent.
- Endure when it is painful.
- Fly when it is time.
- Help others through their process.

Isaiah 40:31 still stands. Those who wait will mount up.

FINAL COMMISSIONING PRAYER

Father, we receive this charge. Teach us to trust completely. Make us a people who honor process. Strengthen leaders with patience. Heal those in crushing seasons. Elevate those ready to emerge. Let this generation understand divine timing. We surrender fully to Your process. In Jesus' name. Amen.

APOSTOLIC PROPHETIC DECREE OVER THE READER

I decree that you will not abandon your process. You will not resent your cocoon. You will not rush your emergence. You will not retreat from altitude. You will trust God completely. And you will fly—for His glory.

Conclusion

The Process Was Worth It

If the caterpillar could speak from the leaf, it would never imagine the sky. If it could reason from its crawling stage, it might resist the cocoon. If it could feel the dissolving inside the chrysalis, it might assume death instead of destiny. But the butterfly proves something powerful: *The process was worth it.* And so is yours.

YOU SURVIVED WHAT WAS MEANT TO SHAPE YOU

There were moments you thought you would not make it. Moments when the silence was suffocating. Moments when the crushing felt unbearable. Moments when you questioned your calling. Moments when you wondered if God had forgotten you. But you are still here.

Psalm 124:1–2 declares: **"If it had not been the Lord who was on our side…"**

If it had not been for God, the crushing would have crushed you completely. But instead, it refined you. The cocoon did not bury you; it built you. The breaking did not destroy you; it defined you. The silence did not abandon you; it aligned you.

YOU ARE NOT WHO YOU USED TO BE

Something shifted. You pray differently now. You think differently now. You discern differently now. You endure differently now.

2 Corinthians 5:17 says: **"If any man be in Christ, he is a new creature."**

Transformation is not cosmetic; it is cellular. Just as the caterpillar's internal structure was completely reconstructed, God has restructured you:

- Your confidence is deeper.
- Your faith is stronger.
- Your obedience is more intentional.
- Your humility is more genuine.

You do not respond like you used to. You do not panic like you used to. You do not chase what you used to because the process changed you.

THE PAIN HAD PURPOSE

Romans 8:18 reminds us: **"For I reckon that the sufferings of this present time are not worthy to be compared with the glory which shall be revealed in us."**

Not just glory revealed to us; glory revealed in us. Your suffering carved capacity. Your delay developed discipline. Your rejection built resilience. Your waiting cultivated wisdom. The pain was not random; it was instructional. God was not punishing you; He was preparing you.

TRUST HIM AGAIN

This book is not just about one season of transformation; it is about a lifestyle of trust because even butterflies lay eggs that begin new cycles. Growth never stops. There will be new leaves. New seasons. New stretchings. New transformations. And each time, the same invitation will echo: *Trust Me.*

Proverbs 3:5 still applies. **Habakkuk 2:3** still stands. **Isaiah 40:31** still promises. Trust again.

A WORD TO THE ONE STILL IN THE COCOON

If you are still in process as you read this: *Do not quit.*

Galatians 6:9 says: **"Let us not be weary in well doing: for in due season we shall reap, if we faint not."**

Due season is coming. The struggle you feel is strengthening your wings. The silence you hear is shaping your spirit. The darkness you experience is incubating destiny. Stay in the cocoon. God finishes what He starts. **Philippians 1:6** assures you of that.

A WORD TO LEADERS AND THE CHURCH

Church of the Living God — we must return to honoring the process. We must stop promoting charisma without character. We must stop rushing callings without formation. We must disciple patiently. We must shepherd compassionately. We must allow God to mature people before we platform them.

1 Samuel 16:7 reminds us: **"Man looketh on the outward appearance, but the Lord looketh on the heart."**

God develops hearts before He displays platforms. If the church honors the cocoon, it will raise strong butterflies. If leaders trust divine timing, they will build a sustainable revival.

THE SKY IS NOT THE GOAL, OBEDIENCE IS

The butterfly does not fly for applause; it flies because it was created to. Your goal is not visibility; it is obedience. Whether crawling, hidden, emerging or soaring: *Obey.*

Micah 6:8 says: **"What doth the Lord require of thee, but to do justly, and to love mercy, and to walk humbly with thy God?"**

Humility sustains altitude. Obedience sustains anointing. Trust sustains transformation.

ONE FINAL TRUTH

You were never stuck; you were becoming. You were never forgotten; you were forming. You were never buried; you were being rebuilt. The cocoon was not your coffin; it was your construction site. And now…you have wings.

FINAL PRAYER OF COMPLETION

Father, thank You for every stage. Thank You for the crawling, the cocoon, the crushing, the silence, the emergence, and the soaring. Forgive us for the times we resisted what You were refining. Forgive us for the moments we doubted Your design. Today we declare full surrender to Your process. Shape us. Break us if necessary. Rebuild us completely. Elevate us when ready. Use us for Your glory. Let our lives testify that trusting You is never wasted. In Jesus' name. Amen.

FINAL PROPHETIC DECREE

I decree over every reader: You will not abandon the process. You will not resent the crushing. You will not rush your emergence. You will not shrink from altitude. You will trust God completely. And when you fly, you will fly with humility, you will fly with purpose, you will fly with power, and you will help others rise. The process was worth it. Now soar.